★ THE ★
UNITED
STATES
PRESIDENTS

LYNDON B. JOHNSON

Megan M. Gunderson

**Checkerboard
Library**

An Imprint of Abdo Publishing
abdobooks.com

★   ★   ★

ABDOBOOKS.COM

Published by Abdo Publishing, a division of ABDO, PO Box 398166, Minneapolis, Minnesota 55439. Copyright © 2021 by Abdo Consulting Group, Inc. International copyrights reserved in all countries. No part of this book may be reproduced in any form without written permission from the publisher. Checkerboard Library™ is a trademark and logo of Abdo Publishing.

Printed in the United States of America, North Mankato, Minnesota
052020
092020

THIS BOOK CONTAINS
RECYCLED MATERIALS

Design: Emily O'Malley, Kelly Doudna, Mighty Media, Inc.
Production: Mighty Media, Inc.
Editor: Liz Salzmann

Cover Photograph: Lyndon Baines Johnson Library and Museum
Interior Photographs: Albert de Bruijn/iStockphoto, p. 37; AP Images, pp. 6, 7 (with JFK), 15, 16, 19, 36; Frank Wolfe/Lyndon Baines Johnson Library and Museum, p. 29; Getty Images, p. 21; Library of Congress, p. 40; Lyndon Baines Johnson Library and Museum, pp. 5, 6 (family), 7 (oath of office), 11, 13, 20, 23, 25, 27, 28, 31, 33; National Archives, p. 22; Pete Souza/Flickr, p. 44; Shutterstock Images, pp. 7, 32, 38, 39; Wikimedia Commons, pp. 40 (George Washington), 42

Library of Congress Control Number: 2019956442

Publisher's Cataloging-in-Publication Data
Names: Gunderson, Megan M., author.
Title: Lyndon B. Johnson / by Megan M. Gunderson
Description: Minneapolis, Minnesota : Abdo Publishing, 2021 | Series: The United States presidents | Includes online resources and index.
Identifiers: ISBN 9781532193606 (lib. bdg.) | ISBN 9781098212247 (ebook)
Subjects: LCSH: Johnson, Lyndon B. (Lyndon Baines), 1908-1973--Juvenile literature. | Presidents--Biography--Juvenile literature. | Presidents--United States--History--Juvenile literature. | Legislators--United States--Biography--Juvenile literature. | Politics and government--Biography--Juvenile literature.
Classification: DDC 973.923092--dc23

★ CONTENTS ★

Lyndon B. Johnson

At 2:38 p.m. on November 22, 1963, Lyndon B. Johnson became the thirty-sixth US president. The new president took the oath of office on the presidential airplane, Air Force One. It was unlike any other **inauguration**.

Less than two hours earlier, President John F. Kennedy had been **assassinated**. He had been riding through downtown Dallas, Texas. There, he had been shot.

The entire nation was in shock over the loss of its president. Later that day, Air Force One landed at Andrews Air Force Base near Washington, DC. There, Johnson said, "This is a sad time for all people. We have suffered a loss that cannot be weighed." He added, "I will do my best. That is all I can do. I ask for your help—and God's."

As president, Johnson carried out many of Kennedy's plans for the nation. His popularity soared. In 1964, Americans elected Johnson to a full term. He successfully started many of his own programs. However, Johnson could not bring an end to the **Vietnam War**. He did not run for another term. Instead, Johnson retired to his ranch in Texas.

TIMELINE

1908

On August 27, Lyndon Baines Johnson was born near Stonewall, Texas.

1934

On November 17, Johnson married Claudia Alta "Lady Bird" Taylor.

1937

Johnson was elected to the US House of Representatives.

1944

Johnson's daughter Lynda Bird was born.

1931

Johnson moved to Washington, DC, to work for Representative Richard M. Kleberg.

1935

Johnson became director of the National Youth Administration in Texas.

1947

Johnson's daughter Luci Baines was born.

1941

Johnson began serving in World War II.

1963

On November 22, President Kennedy was assassinated. Johnson became president.

1968

On March 31, President Johnson declared he would not run for reelection.

1966

Johnson appointed the first African American head of a cabinet department, Robert C. Weaver.

1973

On January 22, Lyndon B. Johnson died of a heart attack.

1948

Johnson was elected to the US Senate.

★ ★　　　★　　★ ★ ★　　　　　★　　★ ★

1960

Johnson was elected vice president under John F. Kennedy.

1967

Johnson appointed the first African American Supreme Court justice, Thurgood Marshall.

1971

Johnson's book *The Vantage Point: Perspectives of the Presidency, 1963–1969* was published. The Lyndon Baines Johnson Library and Museum was dedicated.

1964

On July 2, President Johnson signed the Civil Rights Act. Johnson was elected president.

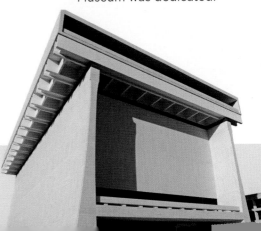

"A President's hardest task
is not to do what is right,

**but to know
what is right."**

Lyndon B. Johnson

DID YOU KNOW?

★ When Lyndon B. Johnson was born, his grandfather Samuel Ealy Johnson Sr. said, "He'll be a United States senator some day."

★ The entire Johnson family had the same initials. *LBJ* stood for Lyndon Baines Johnson and Lady Bird Johnson. It also stood for their daughters, Lynda Bird Johnson and Luci Baines Johnson.

★ The Lyndon B. Johnson National Historical Park includes Johnson's birthplace and his childhood home.

★ The Manned Spacecraft Center in Houston, Texas, is now called the Lyndon B. Johnson Space Center. It was renamed in 1973 in honor of Johnson's support of the space program.

Growing Up

Lyndon Baines Johnson was born on August 27, 1908, near Stonewall, Texas. He was the oldest of five children. Lyndon's parents were Samuel Ealy Johnson Jr. and Rebekah Baines Johnson.

Samuel was a farmer and a schoolteacher. He also was a member of the Texas House of Representatives. Rebekah had graduated from Baylor University in Waco, Texas. She had also been a teacher before she married.

When Lyndon was five, his family moved to Johnson City, Texas. Lyndon's grandfather had been one of the town founders. Growing up, Lyndon did various jobs to help support the family. He shined shoes in the barbershop. And, he herded goats for ranchers.

In school, Lyndon was an average student. He did not like studying, but he earned good grades. Lyndon was better

FAST FACTS

BORN: August 27, 1908

WIFE: Claudia Alta "Lady Bird" Taylor (1912–2007)

CHILDREN: 2

POLITICAL PARTY: Democrat

AGE AT INAUGURATION: 55

YEARS SERVED: 1963–1969

VICE PRESIDENT: Hubert H. Humphrey

DIED: January 22, 1973, age 64

known for his leadership skills. He was class president and participated in **debate**.

In 1924, Lyndon graduated from high school. His parents wanted him to go to college, but he disagreed. Instead, Lyndon and some friends headed to California.

There, Lyndon did a variety of jobs. These included picking grapes and working as a law clerk. Yet Lyndon hardly made enough money to buy food. He returned to Johnson City and worked as a road builder. Soon, Lyndon was ready for college.

Rebekah Baines Johnson

Samuel Ealy Johnson Jr.

Teacher and Husband

In 1927, Johnson set out for Southwest Texas State Teachers College in San Marcos, Texas. To help pay for school, he borrowed $75 from the Johnson City bank. Johnson also had part-time jobs. He worked as a janitor, a secretary to the college president, and a door-to-door salesman.

Still, Johnson could not meet his expenses. So, he left school to earn some money. Johnson got a job as a teacher and principal. He worked at Welhausen School in Cotulla, Texas.

After a year, Johnson returned to college. He graduated in 1930. Soon, he went to Houston, Texas. There, Johnson taught public speaking and **debate** at Sam Houston High School.

Johnson also began helping with Texan Richard M. Kleberg's election campaign. Kleberg won election to the US House of Representatives. He then offered Johnson a job. Johnson moved to Washington, DC, in 1931. There, he worked as Kleberg's legislative assistant for the next four years.

Lynda (*lower left*) and Luci (*upper left*) both married while their father was president.

In 1934, Johnson briefly attended Georgetown University Law School in Washington, DC. The same year, he met Claudia Alta "Lady Bird" Taylor.

The two quickly fell in love. They married within three months, on November 17. The Johnsons had two daughters. Lynda Bird was born in 1944. Luci Baines followed in 1947.

Mrs. Johnson bought an Austin, Texas, radio station called KTBC in 1943. Later, it was renamed KLBJ. Mrs. Johnson was a smart businesswoman, and the Johnsons became wealthy.

Young Politician

In 1935, Johnson became director of the National Youth Administration in Texas. At 26, he was the organization's youngest state director.

Johnson's program gave jobs to students. That way, they could afford to stay in school. It also provided jobs for young people who were not in school. These included **public works** jobs such as building parks, playgrounds, and schools.

In 1937, Johnson was elected to the US House of Representatives. There, he worked to bring electricity to Texans in rural areas. Johnson supported projects for public housing and giving loans to farmers. He also backed soil **conservation** and flood control.

Johnson was a member of the House Naval Affairs Committee. He strongly supported preparing the navy in case of war. Johnson helped plan air training, shipbuilding, and other naval sites in Texas. On December 7, 1941, Japanese forces attacked the US naval base at Pearl Harbor, Hawaii. The United States then entered **World War II**.

During World War II, Johnson served in the Pacific.

Johnson became the first congressman to serve on active duty in the war. For his bravery during the war, he received the Silver Star Medal. In 1942, President Franklin D. Roosevelt ordered all congressmen serving in the war back to Washington, DC. Johnson returned to the House in July.

Johnson first ran for the US Senate in 1941. That year, he lost by just 1,311 votes! He went on to win in 1948, 1954, and 1960.

In 1947, Representative Johnson supported the Taft-Hartley Act. This law protected the rights of workers to organize in unions. It also banned the hiring of only union members. And, it regulated strikes that would cause national emergencies.

Johnson served 12 years in the US House of Representatives. Then in 1948, he ran for the US Senate. Johnson won! There, he served an additional 12 years.

Johnson soon became a **Democratic** Party leader. In 1951, he was elected Democratic **whip**. Two years later, he became Senate **minority leader**. Then in 1955, he became the youngest **majority leader** in Senate history.

On July 2, 1955, Johnson suffered a heart attack. He recovered and returned to the Senate in December. In 1957 and 1960, Johnson helped pass two **civil rights** bills. Both bills concerned voting rights. They were the first civil rights bills passed in more than 80 years.

In 1958, Johnson helped pass the National Aeronautics and Space Act. This formed the National Aeronautics and Space Administration. Johnson continued his work in the Senate for the next two years.

5

Vice President Johnson

In 1960, Johnson campaigned for the **Democratic presidential nomination.** But the Democrats decided John F. Kennedy should run for president instead. They chose Johnson as Kennedy's **running mate.** The **Republican** Party nominated Richard Nixon for president. Henry Cabot Lodge Jr. was his running mate.

Together, Kennedy and Johnson made a good team. Kennedy was from the North, while Johnson was from the South. As a result, both northerners and southerners voted for them.

Kennedy and Johnson won the election. At the same time, Johnson was reelected to the Senate. In January 1961, he took the Senate oath of office. He immediately resigned. Johnson then took the oath of office to become vice president.

Johnson was an active vice president. He attended **cabinet**, National Security Council, and other White House meetings. Johnson was chairman of the National Aeronautics and Space Council. He was also chairman of the President's Committee on Equal Employment

The Democrats nominated Kennedy for president on July 13, 1960, in Los Angeles, California. Johnson was nominated for vice president the following day.

Opportunity. This group focused on ending racial **discrimination** when hiring workers.

As vice president, Johnson was also in charge of the National Advisory Council for the Peace Corps. The Peace Corps is an organization of American volunteers. They assist people in developing countries with agriculture, health, and education.

Mrs. Johnson (*left*) and Mrs. Kennedy (*right*) stood by Johnson's side as he took the oath of office.

In 1963, Kennedy, Johnson, and their wives traveled to Texas. It was partly to begin working toward the upcoming 1964 election.

On November 22, Kennedy and Johnson rode through Dallas. Kennedy was in the backseat of one car.

Johnson was two cars behind him. Suddenly, gunshots rang out. President Kennedy was hit.

When the shots were fired, a **Secret Service** agent pushed Johnson down. He lay over the vice president until they were safe. Kennedy was later pronounced dead at the hospital. Johnson then boarded Air Force One to return to Washington, DC.

On the airplane, Johnson was sworn in as the thirty-sixth US president. His friend

Lee Harvey Oswald

Sarah T. Hughes administered the oath of office. She was a judge from Dallas.

Lee Harvey Oswald was accused of the **assassination**. However, the 24 year old never made it to court. On November 24, local businessman Jack Ruby killed him.

6

President Johnson

In the weeks following Kennedy's death, Johnson showed strong leadership. He helped calm the nation. President Johnson also worked with Congress to pass important laws.

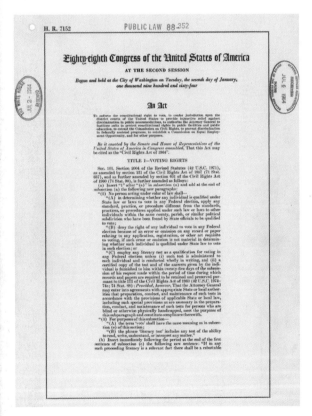

The Civil Rights Act of 1964

On July 2, 1964, President Johnson signed the historic **Civil Rights** Act. It banned **discrimination** in public places. And, it guaranteed equal voting rights. The act also pushed for the **desegregation** of schools. It allowed the government to hold back money from schools that practiced discrimination.

Johnson worked on laws that would help the poor and support education. He also signed a large tax cut. By now, most of Kennedy's policies had passed. Johnson began working on his own programs.

President Johnson signing the Civil Rights Act of 1964

Meanwhile, there was trouble in Asia. Back in 1954, Vietnam had been divided in two. North Vietnam was Communist. South Vietnam was not.

Elections were planned for 1956 to reunite the countries. But South Vietnam's leader, Ngo Dinh Diem, had refused to participate. The United States had supported his decision.

However, North Vietnam had then attacked South Vietnam. America supported South Vietnam. President Dwight D. Eisenhower and President Kennedy had each helped. They had sent money and military advisers.

Then on August 2 and 4, 1964, North Vietnamese ships attacked two American destroyers. The attack occurred off the coast of North Vietnam in the Gulf of Tonkin. Now, the United States became more involved in the conflict. It became known as the **Vietnam War**.

On August 7, Congress passed the Gulf of Tonkin Resolution. It gave President Johnson the power to prevent and defend against attacks by North Vietnam. This allowed the United States to enter the conflict without officially declaring war. Johnson quickly began sending more American troops to fight.

SUPREME COURT APPOINTMENTS

ABE FORTAS: 1965

THURGOOD MARSHALL: 1967

Johnson visited South Vietnam in
1961 while vice president. In 1966, he
traveled there again as president.

PRESIDENT JOHNSON'S CABINET

FIRST TERM

November 22, 1963–January 20, 1965

- ★ **STATE:** Dean Rusk
- ★ **TREASURY:** C. Douglas Dillon
- ★ **DEFENSE:** Robert S. McNamara
- ★ **ATTORNEY GENERAL:** Robert F. Kennedy
- ★ **INTERIOR:** Stewart L. Udall
- ★ **AGRICULTURE:** Orville L. Freeman
- ★ **COMMERCE:** Luther H. Hodges
- ★ **LABOR:** W. Willard Wirtz
- ★ **HEALTH, EDUCATION, AND WELFARE:**
  Anthony J. Celebrezze

SECOND TERM

January 20, 1965–January 20, 1969

- ★ **STATE:** Dean Rusk
- ★ **TREASURY:** C. Douglas Dillon
  Henry H. Fowler (from April 1, 1965)
  Joseph W. Barr (from December 23, 1968)
- ★ **DEFENSE:** Robert S. McNamara
  Clark M. Clifford (from March 1, 1968)
- ★ **ATTORNEY GENERAL:**
  Nicholas Debelleville Katzenbach
  Ramsey Clark (from March 10, 1967)
- ★ **INTERIOR:** Stewart L. Udall
- ★ **AGRICULTURE:** Orville L. Freeman
- ★ **COMMERCE:** John T. Connor
  Alexander B. Trowbridge (from June 14, 1967)
  C.R. Smith (from March 6, 1968)
- ★ **LABOR:** W. Willard Wirtz
- ★ **HEALTH, EDUCATION, AND WELFARE:**
  Anthony J. Celebrezze
  John William Gardner (from August 18, 1965)
  Wilbur J. Cohen (from May 9, 1968)
- ★ **HOUSING AND URBAN DEVELOPMENT:**
  Robert C. Weaver (from January 18, 1966)
  Robert Coldwell Wood (from January 7, 1969)
- ★ **TRANSPORTATION:** Alan S. Boyd (from
  January 16, 1967)

President Lyndon B. Johnson

7

The Great Society

In November 1964, Johnson was elected president. At the time, he won the greatest presidential election victory in US history. He earned 61 percent of the **popular vote**.

Johnson's **running mate** was Minnesota senator Hubert H. Humphrey. They defeated **Republican** candidate Barry M. Goldwater. His running mate was William E. Miller.

Hubert H. Humphrey ran for president in 1968. However, he lost to Richard Nixon.

On January 20, 1965, Johnson was **inaugurated** for his first full term. The previous spring, Johnson had proposed "an end to poverty and racial injustice." He called his plans the Great Society. At his inauguration, Johnson repeated his ideas.

Johnson's Great Society included several programs. Medicare and Medicaid provided health care for the elderly and the poor.

Thurgood Marshall fought for civil
rights throughout his career.

Head Start helped poor children get ready for school. Job
Corps provided job training and other support for youths.

President Johnson also continued to support **civil rights**.
In 1965, he signed the Voting Rights Act. This act further
protected African American voting rights.

In January 1966, Johnson appointed the first African
American head of a **cabinet** department. Robert C. Weaver

became secretary of the Department of Housing and Urban Development. In 1967, Johnson appointed the first African American **Supreme Court justice**, Thurgood Marshall.

At the same time, the **Vietnam War** was going badly. Even with America's help, South Vietnam was struggling. North Vietnam had help from China, another Communist country. Also, many South Vietnamese soldiers were trained by and favored North Vietnam. They used **guerrilla warfare** to fight American and other South Vietnamese forces.

President Johnson sent more and more troops to help South Vietnam. At the beginning of 1968, nearly 500 American soldiers were dying each week. By that time, about 550,000 American soldiers were in the country. At home, Americans protested the war. Johnson's popularity fell quickly.

By early 1968, many Americans believed the war could not end soon. On March 31, Johnson surprised the nation with three announcements. He spoke on television.

Johnson announced a reduction in the bombing of North Vietnam. And, he proposed the opening of peace talks. President Johnson also stated that he would not run for reelection.

In Johnson's televised announcement, he said, "I shall not seek, and I will not accept, the nomination of my party for another term as your president."

8

Back at the Ranch

January 20, 1969, was Johnson's last day as president. The Johnsons then retired to the LBJ Ranch near Johnson City.

Johnson wrote a book about his time as president. *The Vantage Point: Perspectives of the Presidency, 1963–1969* was published in 1971. That year, the Lyndon Baines Johnson Library and Museum was **dedicated**. It is on the campus of the University of Texas at Austin.

On January 22, 1973, Lyndon B. Johnson died of a heart attack. Just a few weeks later, those still fighting agreed to end the **Vietnam War**.

As president, Johnson showed strong leadership after Kennedy's **assassination**. He signed important **civil rights** acts. And, he started vital social programs. He is also remembered for his part in the Vietnam War.

— Johnson wanted the Lyndon Baines Johnson Library and Museum to help visitors better understand the presidency.

During Johnson's presidency, his ranch
was known as the "Texas White House."

Johnson was a congressman, a senator, a vice president,
and a president. In every office, Lyndon B. Johnson worked
hard to serve his country.

BRANCHES OF GOVERNMENT

The US government is divided into three branches. They are the executive, legislative, and judicial branches. This division is called a separation of powers. Each branch has some power over the others. This is called a system of checks and balances.

★ EXECUTIVE BRANCH

The executive branch enforces laws. It is made up of the president, the vice president, and the president's cabinet. The president represents the United States around the world. He or she oversees relations with other countries and signs treaties. The president signs bills into law and appoints officials and federal judges. He or she also leads the military and manages government workers.

★ LEGISLATIVE BRANCH

The legislative branch makes laws, maintains the military, and regulates trade. It also has the power to declare war. This branch consists of the Senate and the House of Representatives. Together, these two houses make up Congress. Each state has two senators. A state's population determines the number of representatives it has.

★ JUDICIAL BRANCH

The judicial branch interprets laws. It consists of district courts, courts of appeals, and the Supreme Court. District courts try cases. If a person disagrees with a trial's outcome, he or she may appeal. If a court of appeals supports the ruling, a person may appeal to the Supreme Court. The Supreme Court also makes sure that laws follow the US Constitution.

THE PRESIDENT

★ QUALIFICATIONS FOR OFFICE

To be president, a person must meet three requirements. A candidate must be at least 35 years old and a natural-born US citizen. He or she must also have lived in the United States for at least 14 years.

★ ELECTORAL COLLEGE

The US presidential election is an indirect election. Voters from each state choose electors to represent them in the Electoral College. The number of electors from each state is based on the state's population. Each elector has one electoral vote. Electors are pledged to cast their vote for the candidate who receives the highest number of popular votes in their state. A candidate must receive the majority of Electoral College votes to win.

★ TERM OF OFFICE

Each president may be elected to two four-year terms. Sometimes, a president may only be elected once. This happens if he or she served more than two years of the previous president's term.

The presidential election is held on the Tuesday after the first Monday in November. The president is sworn in on January 20 of the following year. At that time, he or she takes the oath of office:

> *I do solemnly swear (or affirm) that I will faithfully execute the office of President of the United States, and will to the best of my ability, preserve, protect and defend the Constitution of the United States.*

LINE OF SUCCESSION

The Presidential Succession Act of 1947 defines who becomes president if the president cannot serve. The vice president is first in the line of succession. Next are the Speaker of the House and the President Pro Tempore of the Senate. If none of these individuals is able to serve, the office falls to the president's cabinet members. They would take office in the order in which each department was created:

Secretary of State

Secretary of the Treasury

Secretary of Defense

Attorney General

Secretary of the Interior

Secretary of Agriculture

Secretary of Commerce

Secretary of Labor

Secretary of Health and Human Services

Secretary of Housing and Urban Development

Secretary of Transportation

Secretary of Energy

Secretary of Education

Secretary of Veterans Affairs

Secretary of Homeland Security

While in office, the president receives a salary of $400,000 each year. He or she lives in the White House and has 24-hour Secret Service protection.

The president may travel on a Boeing 747 jet called Air Force One. The airplane can accommodate 76 passengers. It has kitchens, a dining room, sleeping areas, and a conference room. It also has fully equipped offices with the latest communications systems. Air Force One can fly halfway around the world before needing to refuel. It can even refuel in flight!

Air Force One

If the president wishes to travel by car, he or she uses Cadillac One. It has been modified with heavy armor and communications systems. The president takes

Cadillac One

Cadillac One along when visiting other countries if secure transportation will be needed.

The president also travels on a helicopter called Marine One. Like the presidential car, Marine One accompanies the president when traveling abroad if necessary.

Sometimes, the president needs to get away and relax with family and friends. Camp David is the official presidential retreat. It is located in the cool, wooded mountains of Maryland. The US Navy maintains the retreat, and the US Marine Corps keeps it secure. The camp offers swimming, tennis, golf, and hiking.

When the president leaves office, he or she receives lifetime Secret Service protection. He or she also receives a yearly pension of $207,800 and funding for office space, supplies, and staff.

Marine One

George Washington

Abraham Lincoln

Theodore Roosevelt

	PRESIDENT	PARTY	TOOK OFFICE
1	George Washington	None	April 30, 1789
2	John Adams	Federalist	March 4, 1797
3	Thomas Jefferson	Democratic-Republican	March 4, 1801
4	James Madison	Democratic-Republican	March 4, 1809
5	James Monroe	Democratic-Republican	March 4, 1817
6	John Quincy Adams	Democratic-Republican	March 4, 1825
7	Andrew Jackson	Democrat	March 4, 1829
8	Martin Van Buren	Democrat	March 4, 1837
9	William H. Harrison	Whig	March 4, 1841
10	John Tyler	Whig	April 6, 1841
11	James K. Polk	Democrat	March 4, 1845
12	Zachary Taylor	Whig	March 5, 1849
13	Millard Fillmore	Whig	July 10, 1850
14	Franklin Pierce	Democrat	March 4, 1853
15	James Buchanan	Democrat	March 4, 1857
16	Abraham Lincoln	Republican	March 4, 1861
17	Andrew Johnson	Democrat	April 15, 1865
18	Ulysses S. Grant	Republican	March 4, 1869
19	Rutherford B. Hayes	Republican	March 3, 1877

THEIR TERMS ★

LEFT OFFICE	TERMS SERVED	VICE PRESIDENT
March 4, 1797	Two	John Adams
March 4, 1801	One	Thomas Jefferson
March 4, 1809	Two	Aaron Burr, George Clinton
March 4, 1817	Two	George Clinton, Elbridge Gerry
March 4, 1825	Two	Daniel D. Tompkins
March 4, 1829	One	John C. Calhoun
March 4, 1837	Two	John C. Calhoun, Martin Van Buren
March 4, 1841	One	Richard M. Johnson
April 4, 1841	Died During First Term	John Tyler
March 4, 1845	Completed Harrison's Term	Office Vacant
March 4, 1849	One	George M. Dallas
July 9, 1850	Died During First Term	Millard Fillmore
March 4, 1853	Completed Taylor's Term	Office Vacant
March 4, 1857	One	William R.D. King
March 4, 1861	One	John C. Breckinridge
April 15, 1865	Served One Term, Died During Second Term	Hannibal Hamlin, Andrew Johnson
March 4, 1869	Completed Lincoln's Second Term	Office Vacant
March 4, 1877	Two	Schuyler Colfax, Henry Wilson
March 4, 1881	One	William A. Wheeler

Franklin D. Roosevelt

John F. Kennedy

Ronald Reagan

	PRESIDENT	PARTY	TOOK OFFICE
20	James A. Garfield	Republican	March 4, 1881
21	Chester Arthur	Republican	September 20, 1881
22	Grover Cleveland	Democrat	March 4, 1885
23	Benjamin Harrison	Republican	March 4, 1889
24	Grover Cleveland	Democrat	March 4, 1893
25	William McKinley	Republican	March 4, 1897
26	Theodore Roosevelt	Republican	September 14, 1901
27	William Taft	Republican	March 4, 1909
28	Woodrow Wilson	Democrat	March 4, 1913
29	Warren G. Harding	Republican	March 4, 1921
30	Calvin Coolidge	Republican	August 3, 1923
31	Herbert Hoover	Republican	March 4, 1929
32	Franklin D. Roosevelt	Democrat	March 4, 1933
33	Harry S. Truman	Democrat	April 12, 1945
34	Dwight D. Eisenhower	Republican	January 20, 1953
35	John F. Kennedy	Democrat	January 20, 1961

LEFT OFFICE	TERMS SERVED	VICE PRESIDENT
September 19, 1881	Died During First Term	Chester Arthur
March 4, 1885	Completed Garfield's Term	Office Vacant
March 4, 1889	One	Thomas A. Hendricks
March 4, 1893	One	Levi P. Morton
March 4, 1897	One	Adlai E. Stevenson
September 14, 1901	Served One Term, Died During Second Term	Garret A. Hobart, Theodore Roosevelt
March 4, 1909	Completed McKinley's Second Term, Served One Term	Office Vacant, Charles Fairbanks
March 4, 1913	One	James S. Sherman
March 4, 1921	Two	Thomas R. Marshall
August 2, 1923	Died During First Term	Calvin Coolidge
March 4, 1929	Completed Harding's Term, Served One Term	Office Vacant, Charles Dawes
March 4, 1933	One	Charles Curtis
April 12, 1945	Served Three Terms, Died During Fourth Term	John Nance Garner, Henry A. Wallace, Harry S. Truman
January 20, 1953	Completed Roosevelt's Fourth Term, Served One Term	Office Vacant, Alben Barkley
January 20, 1961	Two	Richard Nixon
November 22, 1963	Died During First Term	Lyndon B. Johnson

	PRESIDENT	PARTY	TOOK OFFICE
36	Lyndon B. Johnson	Democrat	November 22, 1963
37	Richard Nixon	Republican	January 20, 1969
38	Gerald Ford	Republican	August 9, 1974
39	Jimmy Carter	Democrat	January 20, 1977
40	Ronald Reagan	Republican	January 20, 1981
41	George H.W. Bush	Republican	January 20, 1989
42	Bill Clinton	Democrat	January 20, 1993
43	George W. Bush	Republican	January 20, 2001
44	Barack Obama	Democrat	January 20, 2009
45	Donald Trump	Republican	January 20, 2017

Barack Obama

★ PRESIDENTS MATH GAME ★

Have fun with this presidents math game! First, study the list above and memorize each president's name and number. Then, use math to figure out which president completes each equation below.

1. Lyndon B. Johnson – James K. Polk = ?

2. Andrew Jackson + Lyndon B. Johnson = ?

3. Lyndon B. Johnson + James Monroe = ?

Answers:
1. William McKinley (36 – 11 = 25)
2. George W. Bush (7 + 36 = 43)
3. George H.W. Bush (36 + 5 = 41)

LEFT OFFICE	TERMS SERVED	VICE PRESIDENT
January 20, 1969	Completed Kennedy's Term, Served One Term	Office Vacant, Hubert H. Humphrey
August 9, 1974	Completed First Term, Resigned During Second Term	Spiro T. Agnew, Gerald Ford
January 20, 1977	Completed Nixon's Second Term	Nelson A. Rockefeller
January 20, 1981	One	Walter Mondale
January 20, 1989	Two	George H.W. Bush
January 20, 1993	One	Dan Quayle
January 20, 2001	Two	Al Gore
January 20, 2009	Two	Dick Cheney
January 20, 2017	Two	Joe Biden
		Mike Pence

WRITE TO THE PRESIDENT

You may write to the president at:

**The White House
1600 Pennsylvania Avenue NW
Washington, DC 20500**

You may email the president at:

www.whitehouse.gov/contact

★ GLOSSARY ★

assassinate—to murder a very important person, usually for political reasons. An act of assassinating someone is an assassination.

cabinet—a group of advisers chosen by the president to lead government departments.

civil rights—rights that protect people from unequal treatment or discrimination.

conservation—the planned management of natural resources to protect them from damage or destruction.

debate—a contest in which two sides argue for or against something.

dedicate—to open to public use.

Democrat—a member of the Democratic political party. Democrats believe in social change and strong government.

desegregation (dee-seh-grih-GAY-shuhn)—the elimination of the separation of people based on race.

discrimination (dihs-krih-muh-NAY-shuhn)—unfair treatment based on factors such as a person's race, religion, or gender.

guerrilla warfare (guh-RIL-uh WOR-fair)—a form of war based on making surprise attacks behind enemy lines.

inaugurate (ih-NAW-gyuh-rayt)—to swear into a political office. An act of being inaugurated is an inauguration (ih-naw-gyuh-RAY-shuhn).

justice—a judge on the US Supreme Court.

majority leader—the leader of the party that has the greatest number of votes in a legislative body, such as the US Senate.

minority leader—the leader of a party that does not have the greatest number of votes in a legislative body, such as the US Senate.

popular vote—the vote of the entire body of people with the right to vote.

public works—projects the government pays for, such as roads, dams, or sewers.

Republican—a member of the Republican political party. Republicans are conservative and believe in small government.

running mate—a candidate running for a lower-rank position on an election ticket, especially the candidate for vice president.

Secret Service—a federal law enforcement agency. Its duties include conducting criminal investigations and protecting national leaders, such as the president, and visiting foreign leaders.

Supreme Court—the highest, most powerful court in the United States.

Vietnam War—from 1954 to 1975. A long, failed attempt by the United States to stop North Vietnam from taking over South Vietnam.

whip—a member of a political party who is in charge of making sure party members attend important voting sessions.

World War II—from 1939 to 1945, fought in Europe, Asia, and Africa. Great Britain, France, the United States, the Soviet Union, and their allies were on one side. Germany, Italy, Japan, and their allies were on the other side.

ONLINE RESOURCES

Booklinks
NONFICTION NETWORK
FREE! ONLINE NONFICTION RESOURCES

To learn more about Lyndon B. Johnson, please visit **abdobooklinks.com** or scan this QR code. These links are routinely monitored and updated to provide the most current information available.

★ INDEX ★